Philosophy for children

From child to children

The turtle fix!

From child to children

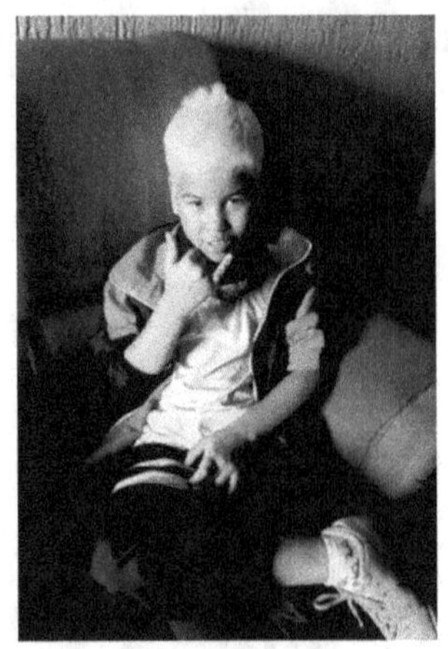

By: Bernardo Octaviano Pereira

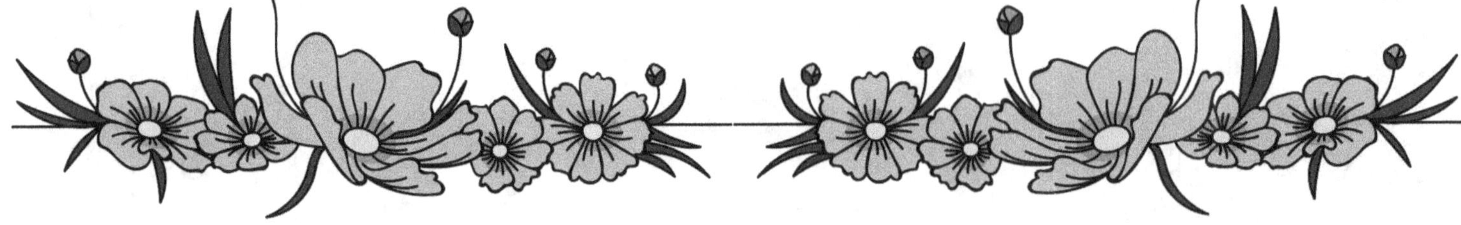

This book belongs to:

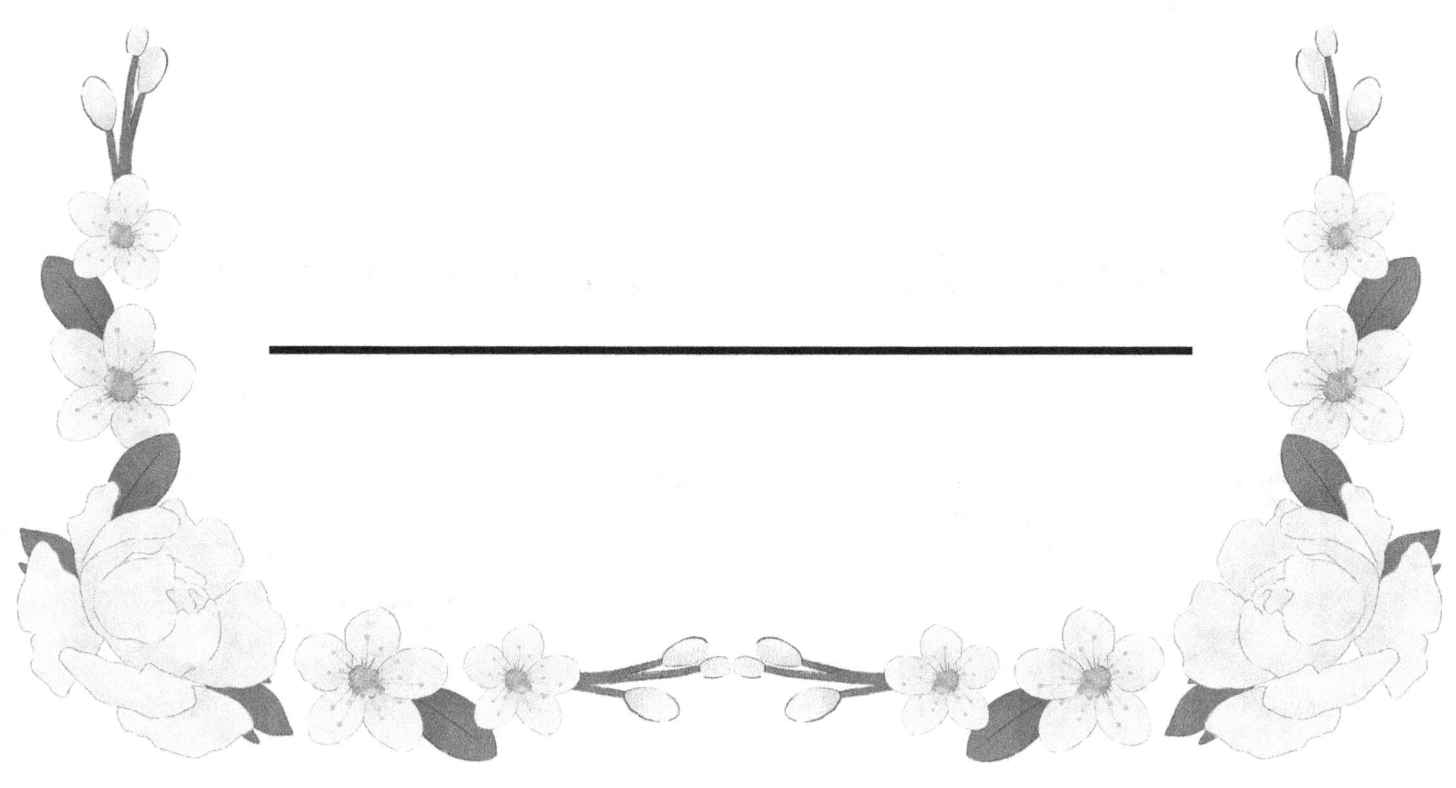

I dedicate this work, firstly, to my parents who I love so much, to my teachers, to my dear aunts and to all my friends, may God bless you all infinitely!

Bernardo Octaviano Pereira

05/04/2024

Once upon a time, in a forest not far from here, there lived a lively group of happy little animals, always playing and singing;

One day there was a little party in heaven that promised, a special celebration, and all the little animals were invited to the party;

There were all the little animals from the forest, the party was really good, lots of food, lots of drinks and good music.

Until an hour later, almost at the end of the party, there was an argument that ended in a fight in the room;

And all the little animals will run in all directions to avoid the confusion,

and
unfortunately
the little turtle
lost its balance
and fell from the
sky, and broke
its entire shell,
leaving it in
several pieces.

And the little turtle was very sad, and cried a lot, that's when daddy from heaven said, don't cry my little girl, I'll help you,

I'm going to glue all the little pieces together, and with skillful hands, daddy in heaven began to carefully glue each little piece of the shell.

As the parts came together, the little turtle's shell was not only restored, but it also gained an even greater beauty than before.

The little turtle, previously sad, was now radiant with happiness, thanking daddy in heaven for his loving intervention.

This story reminds us that even in the most difficult times, there is always a chance for healing and renewal.

Sometimes falling can make us even stronger and more beautiful, and loving help from someone special can make all the difference.

The end!

www.ingramcontent.com/pod-product-compliance
Lightning Source LLC
Chambersburg PA
CBHW081543250726
48659CB00009B/3057